PARTS of *Me*

KIMBERLEY Z. TENT

PARTS of *Me*

Copyright © 2019 KIMBERLEY Z. TENT.
Interior Graphics/Art Credit: Keith Hershmiller

All rights reserved. No part of this book may be used or reproduced by any means, graphic, electronic, or mechanical, including photocopying, recording, taping or by any information storage retrieval system without the written permission of the author except in the case of brief quotations embodied in critical articles and reviews.

Archway Publishing books may be ordered through booksellers or by contacting:

Archway Publishing
1663 Liberty Drive
Bloomington, IN 47403
www.archwaypublishing.com
1 (888) 242-5904

Because of the dynamic nature of the Internet, any web addresses or links contained in this book may have changed since publication and may no longer be valid. The views expressed in this work are solely those of the author and do not necessarily reflect the views of the publisher, and the publisher hereby disclaims any responsibility for them.

Any people depicted in stock imagery provided by Getty Images are models, and such images are being used for illustrative purposes only.
Certain stock imagery © Getty Images.

ISBN: 978-1-4808-7330-8 (sc)
ISBN: 978-1-4808-7331-5 (e)

Library of Congress Control Number: 2019933760

Print information available on the last page.

Archway Publishing rev. date: 04/24/2019

Parts of Me

Dedication
For

My Family

Butch, my Rock and the love of my life, you stood by my side through hell and lifted me up when I could no longer stand on my own. Kaylee, Paige, & Cody, you had confidence in me when I needed it the most! You showered me with unconditional love and support, and you make me so proud to be your mom. Mama Bean, oh how I love you! You taught me to trust and walk with Jesus, no matter the circumstance, and to forgive others even when they can't forgive themselves. Austin, Zackary, & Avery, my precious babies, Grammy loves you so much. Your hugs, giggles, and kisses helped me get up in the morning. Tam, for not giving up on YOU—and for not giving up on ME. Walt, Tommy, & Paula, you mean the world to me, you are family. And to my Papa in Heaven, I feel you here … infinity twice.

For

Crystal, you saved my life. You helped me weed through the crap to see the truth, and to believe in my own worth. My ED/Trauma "Homies," you know who you are—trust the process! And to my Nor, for not leaving my side or the road that day. I love you.

And For

Chris McGee, for not allowing me to prove how tough I was, for saving my ass and sending me to the doctor when it wasn't only my pride hurting. I learned so much from you, MODEL supervisor! My fellow Members, you don't have to hide anymore. You know who you are ...

Being wise
isn't something we grow into.
Not everyone becomes wise.
To become truly wise,
we must lead, and
to lead,
we must not be silent.
It's time to stand up
for our heart's truth and
encourage those close to us
to stand tall as well—
to become leaders,
to be the warriors
we know us to be,
even if that places
our own weakness
on display.
Once upon a time,
there was a Journey …

My Journey.

Contents

... and darkness clung to light 1
   Dear Parts, ... 3

Broken 7
   Hidden War 8
   Lost Soul 10
   To Die a Thousand Times 12
   Body on the Floor 14
   Member Down 16
   A Painted Tragedy 17
   Hopeless 19
   About Time 21
   Fog 22

Emotions 25
   Nobody's Fault 27
   Wasted Time 28
   Poor Man's Bottle 29
   A Dozen Swords 30
   House with no Flowers 31
   Mirror, Mirror 33
   Reflection 35
   When Darkness Falls 36
   Child of Mine 37
   Shame 39
   The Red Soldier 40

Healing 45

    E.D. 47
    Sweet Nectar 48
    Wooden Crown 50
    Reckoning 52
    Leaving Her 56
    No Hurry 57
    Slumber 58
    Unspoken Irony 59
    Beautiful Vagrant 60
    Goodbye 62

Hope 65

    Surrender 69
    On Bended Knee 70
    Senseless 73
    The Choice 74
    Peace 76
    Safe Place 79

Belief 81

    Inner Leader 84
    Yellow Stripes 86
    Emmy 87
    Letter to My Love 89

... and darkness clung to light

Dear Parts,

I never saw you coming. I never heard a sound ... but I felt you. I remember the night you first whispered, "I've got your back." I remember the twisted wire pulling tighter and tighter around my head, bones breaking, and the taste of metallic liquid on my tongue. I remember wicked black eyes and a fierce intention of survival—even then, I felt your presence cling to my back. I know now, that I never stood a chance. Showing yourself to me as a Hero was secretly sacrificial ... humbling and yet, a betrayal all the same.

I practiced cutting the steel, seeking freedom nightly from the bottomless pit of hell and failing. I clung to the hope that when the moment came, I'd be well versed in survival and that death would wait once more. You repeatedly showed me the grim results at 3:26 am, and when time—once again—shut the door in my face ... you were there.

You offered me hope as I stood naked before that floor-to-ceiling mirror. You were there when I choked on life, you lifted me up when I pleaded for clemency ... you became a shadow, never leaving my side, teasing me with your truth, yet ridiculing my devotion.

I became a studied Warrior, clothed in gaunt flesh, with a burning gut and taxed memories. You suspended food before my eyes and encouraged me to gorge on its richness, only to witness it being cast from my belly, like yesterday's trash. Week by week, year by year, you taunted me with loyalty, your intentions eventually revealing an unjust truth: I could no longer survive without you.

You became a refuge of sorts, a strength and my soulmate. You showed me that I could depend on you, bound as I was by fear and penitence, without testament. You forgave me my secret plans for your demise and reminded me, that in you, I could find happiness, acceptance, and beauty. I never questioned your truth—your intentions seemed clear. You saved me, and I owed you that much, or so I thought.

Years later, we met face to face. As I lay, soul dying, face down in a sea of two-inch Persian threads, you revealed your true design: YOU, with a false face and selfish intention. You wanted me dead. You pleaded with me to trust you and leave behind everyone I loved. I remember that moment all too well ... the same moment that the warm breath of God filled my lungs. I heard you, you know. I heard your voice pleading with me to remember your piety, that I was nothing without you.

You lied.

I chose life and I chose my family. In your place, I reappointed God as my leading light. I vowed that day to share His unconditional love with every person I encounter. That is why I'm writing to you today. You provided me comfort for over six years, stood next to me while I suffered, and I thank you for that. You demanded perfection in place of failure.

I will LIVE, and I will breathe LOVE. I am Worthy, and I will live this journey fully, with purpose, and without you. Goodbye Shame, Self-hatred and Doubt.

And good riddance, Bulimia. I stand here, naked in His truth and ... I'm finally at peace.

Xx,

    Kim

Life as a Police Officer is lonely at times.
    It is tough.
    And it can be deadly.

But,

we are at far greater risk from our own minds,
    our own unrealistic self-expectations,
    than we are from the Public.

Shifts end ...
    our own judgments don't.
    - kt

Broken

Hidden War

I knew you,
your heart torn
by the war inside.
You fought for peace,
in your head.

The darkness
that kept you awake at night,
with charred visions
burned into your flesh.

I knew your wide smile,
though the churning in your gut
silently picked away at your seams.

The anxious bile rising up your throat,
the pulse racing at a room too full of faces.

I knew you, your love for your family,
the tears you wiped away
trying to impossibly digest words of support.

The built-up anger
turned into self-loathing,
and continuous regrets sent
over another impossible outing.

I knew your hidden shame
and the bar you fought valiantly to meet
if only to silence the blackness, for a while.

To live completely
the life you needed and deserved
did not, but for a moment, outweigh
your decision to end the war.

We never met,
but I knew you well.

Lost Soul

My course changed at dusk
one season, the cold air hitting
my nostrils, and the sound of rubber sliding
on a road of glass, static instead of my cry
of warning, on portables not working
and comrades doomed.
Like it was yesterday.

Twisted wires, crisp new snow
and a buried red taillight, still blinking and burning my
eyes, mocking me with unwavering flickers of death and
an ounce of time passing before my eyes, as I feel
the warmth of my own dread, weep through crisp
habit.

I am lost to this moment,
the thief of my existence and long lost
dreams.

Each night my legs refuse to carry my weight,
as I eye the hopeless tangle of smoking rubber and
bent cargo, skating toward me.

Time appears suspended, and
it mocks me with your face,
my precious child.

I linger, only for a moment,
yearning to touch your
cheek, one last time,

but a sweet, sweet sound
calls my name, and
it's finally okay to
say goodbye.

To Die a Thousand Times

You died again last night.
After you were gone, I lay there numb,
my chest pounding, and
I cried for you.
There was no use for sleep as over and over,
I revisited your dying face.
The old, helpless feeling of guilt crept in,
and I wore it for hours. I couldn't save you.
Last night you died ... again.

You died again two nights ago.
I watched your last breath, and
I cried for you to stay, but it was too late,
you were already pale and still.
I held your face in my hands, but it didn't matter.
I didn't feel the heat from the fire or
hear the yells, but no matter.
I couldn't save you.
Two nights ago, you died ... again.

You died again last week.
And after I held you in my arms, I gave up.
The same old shame crept in and consumed my sleep,
as I lay there staring at an empty space above the bed.
I reached out to your reflection and felt only a cold cheek.
I couldn't save you.
Last week you died … again.

You will die again tonight.

Body on the Floor

Blink away the horrors,
step bravely through the door.
There are cracks in the timber
and a body on the floor.

No time to second guess,
better choke down the fear
with eyes staring through the glass,
there's no room for tears.

Blood painted on the ceiling,
a song's playing by a band,
the husband's in the corner,
gun still resting in his hand.

"Daddy?" from a small voice,
pure terror in its tone,
all neck hairs stand on guard,
when it's clear you're not alone.

Barrel steady on its target,
faithful partner to the right,
shallow breathing makes you dizzy,
from a standoff here tonight.

No time for second guessing,
there's a child to now protect.
Do you chance the weight of blame
for a life you now have wrecked?

Blink away the horrors,
step bravely through the door.
There are cracks in the timber,
and a Mommy on the floor.

Member Down

She said it calmly, yesterday
a slight waver in her voice, yet her hand
held steady on the tone.
She knew that time and hope
were not enough this round, yet her training
allowed no defeat.

So, on she surged, adrenaline pounding,
mindless to the growing crowd, yearning for
the lights of red and blue.
The charge in the air, caused
a silent prayer, yet in her head was a belief
that no God was near.

But on she crawled, flesh burning
from whispers and jagged stones, yet willing
her truth to rise.
She called out bravely, yesterday,
with no stripe on cloth, yet a badge still in hand
bearing a numbered face.

Member down, Prince,
Member down.

A Painted Tragedy

Don't leave me in this place
alone, with
the blank faces and hollow
voices.

I stand on the lakeshore
wishing
to hear laughter, first love.
I grow up alone
numb in the line for
free bread.

Don't leave me to sing alone
in this place.
The music has no beat,
and time stops
as I paint your face from memory:

a blank canvas.

broken senses,
untrusting heart,
dark tears on
salted cheeks, chilly
reminders of broken
bone, grim hints
of silver wire,
chipped teeth still etched
in nightly
slumber

Hopeless

I see your face, begging
me to let go.
Come here liquid fire,
I will be your peace.
Sing this song of
happiness
from a day bygone;
go ahead and take
this gun.
No matter now, I
am already gone,
I am already
gone.

The cloud danced
                           silently
   in the sky

        of pure white fluff

                              It floated;
made an image of
   a dog

and a beast with no legs.
                      But dark skies rolled

In
with the thunder and
     the rain
and the little cloud
   was eaten
alive.

About Time

Truth simmers quietly

    under a layer of

        red cloth,

while fear mocks her

    confidence in a

        memory.

Putting on a brave face

    is easier than the

        letting go.

Fog

I couldn't remember your name today.
You, the one I adore the most,
my closest friend.
I couldn't remember the place you live today.
You, the one I conceived,
my firstborn child.
I couldn't remember where you went today.
You, the one I rely on,
my love, my life.
I remember asking when you were leaving
and why you had to go,
just not that I'd already asked three times.
I remember what you said,
I really do,
but now it just slipped my mind,
and I'm sorry.
I'm so sorry that I have forgotten
once again, for
you really do mean so much to me,
my love, my friends.
I may not remember things tomorrow,
how I know you or
where you are from,
but know that I will always
love you, and
remember me please,
    before tomorrow.

Building trust on a

    cracked foundation,

is like

    riding a bike with

a square wheel ...

    In the end,

both require stitches.

Emotions

Nobody's Fault

One instant was all it took
to drain a well full of beauty
into a pit of empty days
and nights.

It's nobody's fault she stumbled.
How could it be, when
the stripes still hung
as the moon coasted down,
and the secret became finely tuned
behind four walls of glass,
when the stream trickled on
as footsteps crushed its bank
and the sun reflected an image,
of a life kept out of sight?

It's nobody's fault she drifted.
How could it be, when
the grade still beamed
as the pressure mounted
and self-preservation outweighed risk
of a shameful mortal fall, in
that one moment.

Wasted Time

I thought of you today, smiled, and
passed on by,
swallowed a familiar brick of guilt,
and again, longed
to save you from the anger,
the bruised reminders of
a father's abomination.

He could not love you then.
Demons rode his back, and stole
your dreams, and
he cannot love you now, buried
beneath sodden clay and leaves,
no breath in your lungs.

I thought of you today, cried, and
passed on by.

Poor Man's Bottle

There is a special place
in my depths
held just for you.
It has many rooms
to welcome you.
It is cushioned by sweet sap
to soften a bad day
and lined with love
to lift and comfort you,
and celebrate each victory
right by your side.
So lean closer to me
and share today's distress.
I am ever faithful
and do not judge your heart.
Reservations are not needed here
my love, for this endless space, in
which you already live …

A Dozen Swords

What

    are

        you

            going

                to

                    do,

                        to

                      not

                gain

            it

        all

back?

House with no Flowers

It sits on the corner
of a dead-end lane;
signs of once regal skin
peek through its layers,
and allow a glimpse
of a house once loved.
It boasts room for faces
of a wilted family tree;
echoes of laughter still whisper
and bounce from wall to wall.

They say a lady once dwelled
inside the grand corner house,
when blossoms as bright as her smile
swayed brilliantly in the breeze,
and trees bore perfectly groomed buds
from a weekly tailored lawn.
But eves of dark and twisted wrath
clung to the seams of her nightshirt,
visions now charred reminders
of an antiquated day.

They say a lady was once loved
in the house with no flowers.

I'm broken,
sobbed the hare.
So am I,
retorted the fox.

I don't know what I want from this life,
cried the hare.
Me neither,
countered the fox.

I'm dying inside,
bleated the hare.
Me too,
admitted the fox.

I'm already gone,
wept the hare.
I'm already gone.

Touché,
whispered the fox …
and ate the hare anyway.

Mirror, Mirror

Is this really born flesh staring back at me?
With darkened eyes and once glowing cheeks
mocking me in a paltry shade of goodbye?
Why does it cover aged, trembling palms,
forcing me to remember a grim script
of tightened wire, darkness, and shame?

I've lost precious pieces of moments passed on,
a beautiful canvas gone blank over time,
with covered limbs and memory fogged.
What does life mean, if it's partially gone,
when jagged scraps are hidden under clay,
of dragons, turmoil, and childish desire?

Beware the sting of promises not kept,
of scarlet tunic treachery and secrets
held above steep ladders of false face,
shadows of timeless abandonment,
chained to the gut of a charcoal box, now
rusted and floating south on a nameless river.

Will I ever recognize the image staring back at me?
the one dreaming of a better place 'round the bend,
and searching for truth in one single day?
Can unconditional love of self truly survive shared air
within a society unjust, or do we surrender ourselves
to daily checks
in bloodstained mirrors?

Left, right
left, right, left. Left, right,
left, right, left.
Chins up, eyes straight and
buttons all in line,
backs stiff, browns gleam, and
a sea of spurs sound in unison,
clink, clink, clink,
about face with steady breath and
hollowed out expression.
Throats swell with reflection,
right palms at brow, to the hips and
eyes peek left, unsteady,
bearing witness to a bride pass by, in
perfectly pressed linen, a child on her arm.
Red and white flag follows behind.
Stand tall when the trumpet sounds, and swallow
all regret, for his truth is finally revealed
from a solid oak crate.

Reflection

I remember when
fire ripped through my chest,
when
there were no limits to my dreams.
When
the wind tousled my hair,
and when
there was no measuring my miles.
I remember when
the ocean invited me in,
and when
there was no holding me back.
When
the mirror smiled back at me,
and when
there was no hatred or fear.
I remember the first time
I lost my way,
and when
there was a cocoon left behind.
But through it all,
I remember most,
the day when
my own reflection
mattered.

When Darkness Falls

Never fear the night,
for the secrets it holds
will clutch the silk web
you desperately weaved.
Hand over your inner peace;
it will toil with
the beating of your heart
and steal your last breath.
Let your imagination wander
and thank the Part
that shows up to the gate,
that feels free to color
a night of fantasy,
when darkness falls.

Child of Mine

Sweet child of mine,
I bid you now goodnight.
Heed my words little one,
before dark turns light.

Sweet child of mine,
dream a simple, pleasant thought.
Reject the charms of evil, for
he your friend, is not.

Sweet child of mine,
I bid you now goodnight.
Heed my words little one,
before dark turns light.

Shame

This coat of fur is heavy
with scars on display, buttons too tight.
How can a person be so close to death,
yet still breathe?
A layer of shame continues to taunt
with daily news of tragedy
and fingers pointed all 'round.
How can humans claim
to understand, yet still judge?
This pretense of joy weighs me down
while shadows creep closer
and wake me with chilly reminders.
How can a person heal when
darkness and death still rule?
A belief in self is still a memory
with shifts bygone
and filled with pride and leadership.
How do I see truth while
horrors still invade my sleep,
still taunt?
This life of honor
is a thankless duty
with wounds loosely stitched
and bared just enough for the enemy to see.
How can a person stand tall
in this coat of red,
but in fact, still be dead?

The Red Soldier

1, 2, 3, and 4,
all broken souls but
still lined up to serve,
on bandaged limbs and
shameful sorrows.

Tears are hidden
in the depths of smiles
and in the shadows,
behind the broken door
of a metal locker stall.

5, 6, 7, and 8,
all see but not one stops
to offer salve for the bruise.
A planted fear lurks within and
still the next rung to climb,

and yet it's questioned
when they fall
one by one, heel to toe,
the truth now buried
under stained soil and foggy veil.

9 and 10, yet again
march with heads held high
fresh smiles and shiny kit,
costly badge in left palm
five digits and a brand-new name,
somehow still conceal
the fallen numbers of
The Red Soldier.

Did you see the metal
twisted around once perfect teeth
or feel the crunch of dirt
and bone between hollow cheeks?
Did you hear the grinding of beans
pureed into mush,
or taste the irony of flesh lost
and a goal obtained by sacrifice?

Did you notice the shiny tool on hand
always plotting in constant wait,
or hear the cries of fear in the night
and the persistent dread of darkness?
Did you feel the bile inching up
to cut off the sole path of wind,
or replay the instant betrayal of self
and try to swallow the memory?

Did you know the girl before
wagering overshadowed her skill
or believe that, at length, time heals
and the blank spaces eventually fill?
Did you truly sense the fear
below the practiced smile
or feel the pangs of hunger
and the reality of uncertainty?

Did you care to speak of terror
behind her four walls of despair
or fall short with lost status
and a friendship proven surface?
Did you know that you failed to see
the truth between gorged lips
or search behind once molten eyes
for absolute surety
and a faultless death?

It's emptiness
    really,

    the sheer pain of

a hollow gut

    ripping out,

    and bile

oh, the bile

    crawling up

    a singed, throbbing

throat.

    It's emptiness

    really, all this truth, this

letting go.

Healing

He told her
    she
        couldn't,
Yet,
    she
        did.

E.D.

I'm sheltered by
a sea of comfort
which rocks me to and fro.
I have a heart,
though not revealed,
it's hidden far below.
I hear you talk
a soft, sweet sound
how distant it is not.
I close my eyes
and picture life,
but darkness fills my thoughts.
Tomorrow I will
show my face,
I'll struggle to get through,
and leave behind
this cozy nest
my first breath, a journey without you.

Sweet Nectar

Sing to me
sweet, sweet child,
let my comfort
nourish the betrayal
of this earth,
of your sire,
of your deepest roots.

Oh, weep on me
my sad, sad child,
your salt tastes like
candied sugar
etching a path
on my neck,
on my inner core.

Hold me close
broken, broken child,
let my forgiveness
weaken the judgment
of your peer,
of your foe,
of your own mind.

Oh, give in to me
my weak, weak child,
let my sweet nectar
soften the throes
of battles lost,
of triumphs bygone, and
of your ultimate
demise.

Wooden Crown

She never chose to wear
the wooden crown,
with curved grains
and chipped rubies.
Nor did she ask to tread
the tide alone,
on weed-wrapped limb,
with stained teeth and
finely manicured toes.
Please meet her at the gate,
don't forget your love lost, for
her petals have wilted,
dried against the breeze and
pieces now lay crumbled
at the bend in the drive.
She never chose the crown
you see,
she never chose.

This wandering
 Spirit
Silently longs
 For
A pillow to call
 Home.

Reckoning

We pass the corner, dusk by dusk.
How can a locale be so severe,
to render passersby unaffected,
while nostrils burn from the stench of
yesterday's syrup, and piddle-soaked garb,
and chins turn away,
with efforts of avoidance perfectly clear,
while a heart beats up from the tar,
of a shared walkway,
where compassion is left in yesterday
with drained social grace,
and stained lips
from our own hypocrisy,
when an act of kindness
reaps no reward,
and the lane is all too fast,
when the choice to self-protect
outweighs basic humanity,
while a soul lays motionless
beneath the wheel,
with scars of higher society
charred into weathered skin, and
where a soup can on its side
bears a wooden nickel
begging to keep up,
yet sentenced to disregard.
We pass the corner, dusk by dusk.

Embrace the young child,
celebrate the wonder,

    the colors, the sparkle
in her eyes, and

travel to places which exist
nightly in her dreams.

    Comfort the sweet girl,
wipe away her tears,

the regret, the pain
from her cheeks, and

    prove that trusting souls exist
in this dark, rooted wood.

Protect the innocent one,
jump into the flames,

    the hunt, the turmoil
of a numbered badge lost, and

shield her from the demons
which mock within.

Truth simmers quietly
    under a layer of
    red cloth,
while fear mocks her
    confidence in a
    memory ...
Putting on a brave face
    is easier than the
    letting go.

Bid farewell

you say?

Oh, how

unceremonious

an affair it would be, if

only my heart

weren't stitched to

the inner hem

of a Red

Serge.

Leaving Her

He watched
her
    fall
    and

a piece of him
p
 l
   u
    n
     g
      e
     d
    shortly
    after.

No Hurry

I'm not hurried
to wear these scars,
to carry burned flesh
across the battlefield,
to trip and fall,
to feel the serrated edge
pierce my spine.
I chose the left
fork in the bloody path,
only to be met
by forbidding demons,
Maestros of fire, all
pleased to exhibit my stitches.
Did the Saints sanction
my demise?
Was it a vast array of garb,
an egocentric thought,
or a result of the
final admission of defeat
in this war?
Am I in a hurry
you ask?
By no means, Foe,
am I hurried
to die.

Slumber

No last breath
to utter silent goodbyes.
A beggar of sleep
I am,
on rumpled, cotton sheets.
Don't toy with me,
lying mind,
spitting shame and
always first in line to mock
distorted images.
Treachery on rewind,
I see you now,
Foe,
and slumber
comes at
last.

Unspoken Irony

She cried,

"I feel left behind."

HE whispered,

"Don't worry child, the world just needs to catch up."

Beautiful Vagrant

I can't smell the grass today.
The wind does though,
it carries
rank likeness of
urine soaked denim, ten-bone
whiskey and stale cologne.

Was he once a truck driver, a
carpenter, or maybe a teacher?
Did he fight at the dinner table,
say grace, or have a favorite
song?

What does he have tucked away in
that tattered old knapsack? His best
shirt? Or maybe
some childhood pictures …

How long has he been there,
all curled up with an arm wrapped
around that bag and tin soup can?
Is he guarding his entire life
savings in there?

He twitches, deep in
slumber, manning the wheel
of his own dream.

We aren't so different, he and
I ... both wearing this tired skin.

So why do I gawk at him from
three stories up,
judging his bag of soiled treasures?

And it hits me.

He's been smelling the grass the
entire time, and it was
me
who got distracted
by the wind.

Goodbye

If we had only one day left,
we would sing so loud
the neighbors would complain, and
we would jump in every puddle
until we fell in.
If we had only that one day,
we would play dress up,
then laugh ourselves silly, and
we would make funny faces
at every car driving by.
If we had only one afternoon left,
we would paint all our nails
the color of the rainbow, and
we would make shapes
out of every cloud drifting by.
If we had only that one afternoon,
we would draw castles
on the walls of your room, and
we would pretend we were princesses
just for that day.
If we had only one night left,
we would count each star
one by one, and
we would wish upon each one
that fell from the sky.
If we had only that one night,
we would talk about our loves ones,
our hopes, our fears, and
we would hold hands all night long,

just because.
And when our day came to an end,
we would say goodbye
to us, forever friends, and
I would always remember the moment
we wished upon a star.

Hope

And in that moment,

she stood naked

before a floor length mirror,

and her reflection

spit promise,

not repugnance.

Checkmate,

wicked fool.

Broken?
    Hell yes, I've been broken …

        yesterday.

           It's a choice, really,

              to stay broken, or

                  piece together the cracks,

                  and allow the glue

                to dry.

Surrender

I will not say it today,
the word that tastes like bitter foam
on my lips and
reeks of rotten leaves
from yesterday.

I will not say it tomorrow,
the word that mocks the inside
of my head and
melts the flesh of my gut
with bile.

Although I said it yesterday,
it is a piece of regret
that has no place
in this heart and
no longer lives here.

I will not say it today.

On Bended Knee

I'm no longer dreaming of that day gone by,
with inner madness weighing on
already broken bones.
There is music dancing in my ears
and drummers beating time on
my head,
singers doing solos and
keyboards playing a harmony of echoes.

This is just like me, to daydream,
to relive that fleck of time, in hopes
of your return,
to run wildly into your arms
and to erase the heavy burdens.
She's not here right now, but will be soon,
the one I pray for each morning
and night, on bended knee.

I have sacrificed my inner child and
lost my purpose along the way.
But I will be here waiting,
just as I promised in my "I do."
For this is the way
love is meant to be,
the way our story goes.

She's not here right now, but
will be soon.

She flew
    on damaged wings,
       clipped by a society of
      hatred and masks,
     but held steadfast
    to her flight
   and her purpose was
revealed.

Dipping and swaying,
I play in the cool night air,
tail feathers glistening,
not a single care.
It carries me left
and then to the right,
demanding control of
a commander in flight.
I chirp to my mate,
"Look, way down there!"
our meal now awaits
outside of its lair.
Teamwork is best
when dinner is close,
to share in the gold,
would be fair, to most.
I tend to my nest
on a pole standing high,
feeding my babies,
then whispering goodbye.
My breast is full
as day turns to night,
with His touch, I'm transformed
into a most beautiful
sight.

Senseless

No tears

    will be shed

        over defeat today.

To weep over

    an inner

      battle

        with no hero in

          the end

          seems fruitless

          to me,

        Pet.

The Choice

As sure as a river
    knows
its course,
    I too, will find my way.
The undertow once
    lied
to my soul,
    snaring me in its current.
Many an angler
    waved
as I drifted by, and
    yet again, I closed my eyes.
Down, down, down, I
    surrendered
my own purpose,
    and drowned in red cloth.
The weight on my
    shoulders
instantly levelled
    and sunk to rocky depths.
The choice to breathe or
    die
was mine alone,
    and I thrashed to the surface.
Oh, the bank mocked
    me

in the distance,
    yet I vowed to fight boldly again.
As sure as a river
    knows
its course,
    I too, will find my way.

Peace

A peace
has come over me
and this little place,
inner happiness passed
by, those weary moments
now, ever so distant.
Something has filled the gap,
it starts the mornings off
and continues through sunset.
It brings so much pleasure
and derives from a source
so unique.

To all those ignorant,
it displays new dreams and wonders,
to whom so devoted
it provides eternity,
but remains powerful,
so kind and optimistic.
It makes me wonder,
Why did I wait so long,
to forgive?
The answer, of course,
is truly beyond us all,
but the lessons learned
make no response
necessary.

If you don't empty

the well, bucket

by bucket,

you won't find

the source

of the tainted

water.

I become

   who

      I think

      I am,

         each morning.

Safe Place

I open my eyes to a sky painted
in lavender and burnt sienna,
a salty breeze across my cheek,
and waves crashing against the rocks.
Gulls circle above,
and kids squeal with delight,
throwing bread scraps into the air.
The warm sand squishes between my toes,
his breath brushes the side of my neck, and
I just know … he is fast asleep.
I have always wished to wake up
here, in this place, in this moment
under this sky, with everyone
I love
right here,
on this little beach
in my dreams …
a safe place.

Belief

Spend all the time you need

in the past, but

be sure to lock the door

on your way out ...

Demons
 hate
 that.

Inner Leader

To stand tall in our bravery
and expose our truth
is not easy.
If what we believe
is not heard,
and we are shamed,
is it fair to craft a noose?
Many who stood among us,
fought to be understood,
and refused
to be shadowed by fear, yet,
still they are buried
beneath sodden moss.
Do we step forward two paces
when a threat is near,
or do we expose
our backs to fear?
The grand battle, you see,
is within us all.
It matters whether we
join the war,
but all the more, if
we are meant
to lead.

Nothing is worth
 the cost of
  giving yourself
  away.
   Nothing.

Yellow Stripes

My friends,

remove the stripe
from your pants at dusk,

for sleep is dark enough on its own,

without lending demons
to the cause.

Emmy

God sent an angel
straight from
Heaven,
one afternoon.
My golden friend,
He knew I was wilted, tattered, and
broken.
He saw the burdens of shame, guilt,
and self-hatred, all trapped
inside my soul, and
He knew, He knew
I needed you.

Not once have you judged the
tears, the anger, and
deafening silence.
Nor did you leave my side, when
I couldn't go on, when
nights turned to days, and
days returned to nights, and still,
I had not slept.
He knew that sending down
His own gift of love,
wrapped in golden fur,
would restore my heart,
my faith. With you,
I am never
alone.

Choose
 something,
and
 conquer it.

Choose another,
 then
conquer it too.

Don't be stale.
 Oh, and grin
doing it.

Letter to My Love

Anywhere this journey takes me
is better than where it began,
and I thank you.
I thank you for holding me, through
the tremors and sleepless nights,
the "it's okay … come here's"
and your refusal to let me go,
when even I, lost hope.
I thank you for keeping confidence,
though it must have ripped your
heart out,
and for giving me the space to heal
on my own terms.
You believed in me, out of duty or not,
I don't really know,
but thank you.
For every time you wanted to hold me,
yet I pushed you away,
and during my own isolation,
you refused
to join the crowd.
Thanks for encouraging me to write again,
to share my passion and love
for this world, even when I didn't think
I deserved to be in it.
Thank you for being the person to pick me up
off the living room floor,
and love me through my demons,
for still loving me and loving us
through this new journey …
and a whole new me.

About Me

I reside in beautiful British Columbia
with my childhood sweetheart
of 34 years. I grew up surrounded by nature
and began writing at a very young age. I
have three amazing children and three
grandchildren, who I adore, and who have been
extremely supportive to me throughout this
Journey. My mission is to spread awareness
of PTSD through my own experience as
a First Responder, and to give hope
and support to fellow Police Officers,
who are still suffering in silence.

Xx Kim

My story wouldn't have been
told without the help of:

Paige Tent:

Design/ Illustration

&

Sarah Liu / Three Fates Editing

Editor

... listen to your heartbeat, daily

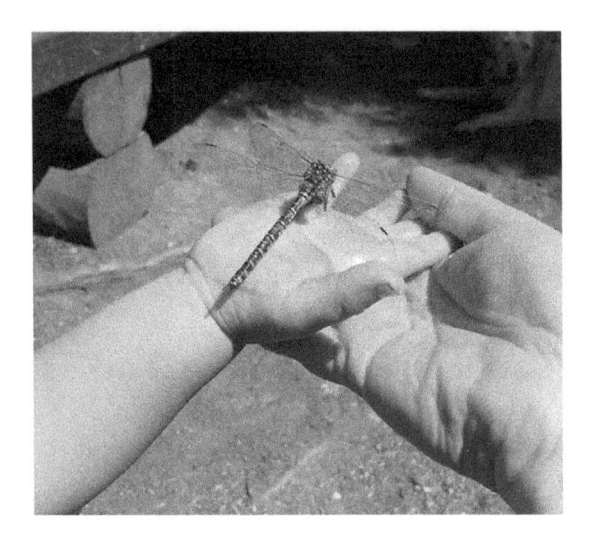

... and out flew the dragonfly

Lightning Source UK Ltd.
Milton Keynes UK
UKHW012031040719
345590UK00001B/9/P